JUN -- 2008

Johns Hopkins:

Poetry and Fiction

John T. Irwin,

General Editor

CIRCUMSTANCES BEYOND OUR

ROBERT PHILLIPS

CONTROL: POEMS

The

Johns Hopkins

University Press

Baltimore

This book has been brought to publication with the generous
assistance of the National Endowment for the Arts and the
Albert Dowling Trust.

The Johns Hopkins University Press
2715 North Charles Street
Baltimore, Maryland 21218-4363
www.press.jhu.edu

Library of Congress Cataloging-in-Publication Data

Phillips, Robert S.
    Circumstances beyond our control : poems / Robert Phillips.
        p. cm.
    ISBN 0-8018-8376-8 (acid-free paper) — ISBN 0-8018-8378-4
(pbk. : acid-free paper)
    I. Title.
    PS 3566.H5C57 2006
    811'.54—dc22   2005024564

A catalog record for this book is available from the British Library.

for Gregory Fraser

and

Rob House,

former students,
fine poets,
constant friends

I don't believe in villains or heroes, only in right
or wrong ways that individuals are taken, not
by choice, but by necessity or by certain still
uncomprehended influences in themselves, their
circumstances and their antecedents.

—Tennessee Williams
New York Post, March 17, 1957

CONTENTS

ACKNOWLEDGMENTS

Thanks to Paula Deitz, Gregory Fraser, Richard Howard, and Wayne Miller for helping revise certain poems. Special thanks to my editor, John T. Irwin, for helping make a final selection from a much larger typescript. And as always, gratitude to my wife, Judith.

Thanks to the following publications, in which some of these poems first appeared, some in earlier versions or with different titles:

Boulevard: "Life Force"

Connecticut Review: "Viewing"

Curbstone Review: "Ghost Story"

Hudson Review: "Famous Last Words" and "Two Adaptations from Red Pine"

Iron Horse Literary Review: "Two for Max Eberts"

Light: The Magazine of Light Verse: "Headlines"

Ontario Review: "Variation on Vallejo's 'Black Stone on a White Stone'" and "The Empty Suit"

Paris Review: "The Ethiopian Eunuch," "The Ocean," and "My Funny Valentine"

Prairie Schooner: "Two Sonnets"

Sewanee Review: "Texas Cheerleader Murder Plot"

Tar River Poetry: "The Grown-up Train"

Western Humanities Review: "The New York Triangle Shirtwaist Factory Fire"

"Ghost Story" appeared in the anthology *Chance of a Ghost,* ed. Gloria Vando

"Arsh Potatoes" appeared in the anthology *Spuds Songs,* ed. Gloria Vando and Robert Stewart

"Christopher Isherwood" was published as a broadside by the Christopher Isherwood Foundation, with a design by Jules White

I   FIRE & OBSESSION

The Ocean

I slam earth again and again,
      and again and again. Not as

a pediatrician slaps a newborn
      to generate first breath, but as

a crazed mother slaps and slaps
      to punish a willful child.

I attack with whatever is at my disposal—
      edges of broken shells, sharp glass

shards, whale bones, driftwood planks.
      I join tropical storms, hurricanes,

I erode, surely but slowly, your
      paltry grassy dunes. They will fall.

I send jellyfish to sting, octopi
      to strangle, sharks with awful jaws.

I ingest poor fishermen, handsome sailors,
      I riptide scuba divers, grandchildren.

I erode edifices of affluence
      built—with effrontery—within my gaze.

Remember, I sank fabulous Atlantis!
      Remember, I took the *Titanic* with one thud!

In contempt, I sometimes return
        a single sneaker or a drowned swimmer.

I will win. Already I possess three-quarters
        of your surface. I will not be ignored.

Ghost Story

The one to whom he always felt most close
died, and he could never comprehend why
he felt no loss, no grief, shed not one tear.
He kept her picture close by, a souvenir
of times past, foreign, even a bit quaint.
And years went by and still he felt that way
until one night, a party, she was there
(this was in a dream, but more real than real).
More beautiful than she had been in life,
dressed to the nines, she mingled, made small talk,
and eventually came over to him:
"I've been missing you every single day,"
she said. His tears released, she went away.

The Grown-up Train

We're on the grown-up train, and we don't get off until the
graveyard.—Matthew Klam, "European Wedding"

We try to maintain adult expressions, as we gaze
    out the train window or read the Financial section
    of the *New York Times.* There are no funny papers
      in the *Times,* which is a good thing—
    we might reveal our ungrownupness.

When the train gets to Chappaqua, we pass kids
    playing baseball in a Little League lot.
    We want to jump off and join them,
    flinging our briefcases, suit coats, laptops,
    and newspapers all over the grass.

We want to hit homers from both sides of the plate.
    We want to barehand a double off the wall,
    allow no base runners between five innings,
    astound the little bastards inside us.
    But we don't. We're on the grown-up train.

We think of mortgages and college tuition loans,
    auto payments and major orthodonture,
    broken-down furnaces and alimony,
    snowplow service and losing our jobs.
    We're on the grown-up train.

An Empty Suit

You can tell he was a big man,
46 Long, sleeves that would hang
below your knuckles, back vent
that would flap below your butt.

You can tell by the fine Italian wool
and cut he was a stylish man.
Not some mail-order or Sears suit,
but a designer label from Neiman's.

You can tell he preferred the subtle:
fabric a minuscule tic-weave,
shaded a smoky dove gray,
any color tie would go with it.

You can tell by the hair-oil stain
inside the back collar he was vain,
or at least well-groomed, a man
for whom appearances mattered.

You can tell he was a smoker,
or socialized with one—two tiny
cigarette burns, one on the right sleeve,
one by the middle button.

You can tell by the small gray stain
to the left of the breast pocket
he hadn't had much time lately
to attend to the dry cleaner's.

You can tell by the frayed bottoms
of the trousers he had lost a lot
of weight. They had drooped
till he was walking on his cuffs.

You can tell by the two red pills
in the right-hand jacket pocket—
potent prescription-strength
for pain—he underwent some ordeal.

You hope that's a lipstick smudge
high on the pearl gray silk lining;
maybe he was loved by somebody
who saw him through, you can't tell who.

But you can tell by the fact it hangs
in the thrift shop here, it isn't
the suit he was laid out in,
that once lucky, now unlucky stiff.

Expulsion

Etching, by Lars Bo, 1962
for Elinor and Jim

Paradise: a Persian word meaning "walled garden."
And the eastward-facing Edenic plot is fenced in
like a rich man's compound. What's the point
of the points on the fence? No one's out there to try
to climb in. Marble lions top posts like bookends.
The garden is circular, overgrown with trees,
including the Tree of Knowledge, lifting limbs
in supplication. Somewhere the subtle serpent lies.

Suddenly the wrought-iron gate swings open
between stone stanchions. From out of the forest
soar myriad fowl, making their own expulsions
in formations like swallows, some large as pelicans,
all ghostly white, as if already grieving their loss.
In the far right-hand corner the beguiled couple
exit. She faces the future, he looks back.
But after this, there is no looking back.

The Snow Queen

for A. S. Byatt

Her bedchamber is white
as a refrigerator, cold
all year as a meat locker.

No meat there. The canopy
over her four-poster bed
is hung with white lace

intricate as snowflakes.
Her windows are frosted,
to keep out the dazzle

of the Northern Lights,
the fun of polar bears
dancing on hind legs.

When she pads barefoot
she never feels the carpet's tickle.
Her nightgown

is white as a winding sheet.
Underneath her pillow
she keeps an icicle,

just in case. Her sheets
are ice floes—white on white—
no cherries in the snow.

She is married to Winter.
It isn't as though she were
locked away by a cold groom.

He'd melt like a snowman
all over that shag carpet,
if she would just let him in.

Life Force

for Eric Luís Brown

It rose like an egg yolk
separated from the white.
Or like the eye of a daisy,
the day's eye. Of course
it was round, a caution
light dangling overhead.
At noon its power bore down,
a runaway school bus.
Clouds were tinged with saffron,
grated lemon rind. When it set,
the horizon became a hotdog
smeared with mustard.

Homage: Neruda

I
Ode to a Banana
for Jules White

Banana, color of the sun,
happy fruit—curved like a smile—
a sunscape, shape of the hunger-
moon, moon hunger, shape of the boom-
erang, smooth golden scimitar,
your hip is the full curve
of my love's hips, your shape
the shape of my arousal.
Banana, your waxy sheath is
an uncircumcised shegitz,
your hacked-off stump
a Thalidomide baby's arm.

I peel back your skin,
revealing your banananess,
your banana-being. Odoriferous
as honeysuckle, lined with corduroy,
stringy, sliced you become shekels,
coins of the realm. Ripe meat
soft as polenta, sweet as roasted
chestnuts, you are chockablock
with potassium. Cut unripe,
you are green, near-tasteless.
Aging, you develop liver spots,
speckled backs of aging hands.

The Hindus believe you
were the fruit forbidden
to Adam and Eve. Your serrated
leaves covered their abject
nakedness. One bunch of you,
banana, can contain two-hundred
bananas. As Livingston's Stanley
exclaimed, "Long after there is no more
wheat, long after there is
no more barley, long after
there is no more rice,
banana, you will feed us."

II
After Reading *The Book of Questions*

Who tells summer it is time to hang out
its yellowed underwear?

Do you know what the earth
dreams about when it hibernates?

In winter does the robin dream
of returning to your backyard?

Are your dreams digital?
Where do they go when you awaken?

And do the poor keep their dreams
stuffed beneath their mattresses?

What makes the trees so happy,
that their leaves dance in the spring?

How does an orange know it is
an orange, and how to taste like one?

How long have the mumbling waves
been conversing with the seashells?

What do you call a tree that moves
from squirrel to squirrel?

When the cat catches a mouse,
do the surviving mice grieve?

Was that prolonged noise in the night
a party given by the peach pits?

Have you ever heard a giraffe sing,
or seen a hippo dance?
Is quicksand a judgment,
or the earth embracing a lover?

What beverage does Jeffrey Dahmer
drink in hell—boy-blood?
Won't death, in the end, be
an interminable case of insomnia?

Variation on Vallejo's "Black Stone on a White Stone"

—Me moriré en París con aquacero . . .

I will die in Houston in the jungle heat,
in air-conditioned air. I already know the date.
I will die in Houston an amber afternoon,
a Thursday—that nothing day—in August,
that dog-days month, when even the grass is depressed.

I will toy with a poem at my antique desk,
attempting something new, doing it badly,
but at least working, trying to see myself
alone, and I am, except for my Siamese cat
lying supine, soporific in a patch of sunlight.

Robert Phillips is dead. When he assayed
to extricate a book wedged in his overloaded
bookcase, the case fell upon him like a tower,
pinned him underneath in a tomb of hardbacks.
His Siamese stood by the cooling body for hours.

On the Interstate eighteen-wheelers smogged
the urban air. His wife came, said undoubtedly
he died happily, scribbling, then reaching for
a favorite book, getting through August in Houston—
the loneliness, the vaporous heat, the humility.

Triangle Shirtwaist Factory Fire

1911

I, Rose Rosenfeld, am one of the workers
who survived. Before the inferno broke out,
factory doors had been locked by the owners,

> to keep us at our sewing machines,
> to keep us from stealing scraps of cloth.
> I said to myself, What are the bosses doing?
> I knew they would save themselves.

I left my big-button-attacher machine,
climbed the iron stairs to the tenth floor
where their offices were. From the landing window

> I saw girls in shirtwaists flying by,
> Catherine wheels projected like Zeppelins
> out open windows, then plunging downward,
> sighing skirts open parasols on fire.

I found the big shots stuffing themselves
into the freight elevator going to the roof.
I squeezed in. While our girls were falling,

> we ascended like ashes. Firemen
> yanked us onto the next-door roof.
> I sank to the tarpaper, sobbed for
> one-hundred forty-six comrades dying

or dead down below. One was Rebecca,
my only close friend, a forewoman kind to workers.
Like the others, she burned like a prism.

Relatives of twenty-three victims later
    brought suits.
Each family was awarded seventy-five dollars.
It was like the *Titanic* the very next year—
No one cared about the souls in steerage.

Those doors were locked, too, a sweatshop at sea.
They died due to ice, not fire. I live in
Southern California now. But I still see

    skirts rippling like parachutes,
    girls hit the cobblestones, smell smoke,
    burnt flesh, girls cracking like cheap buttons,
    disappearing like so many dropped stitches.

Two Twentieth-Century American Monologues

I
Ted Bundy, Stalker Rapist
Gainesville, 1980

The thing of it was,
you looked so handsome
and trustworthy—
such a nice smile.

The thing of it was,
you showed me
a laminated ID card,
said you were Police.

The thing was,
you told me someone
had been arrested
breaking into my car,
did I want to go
down to the station
and press charges?
You'd drive me.

You had a hot car,
smooth, brand new.
Smelled like leather,
a turn-on, like you.

Not far down the road
you pulled over,
quickly handcuffed me,
unzipped yourself,

started waving a pistol,
said you'd blow
my brains all over
the highway if I didn't

do what I was told.
Whatever the reason,
I didn't think you would.
(Your cock was tiny,

soft as a slug.) Somehow
I got the door open,
ran. You didn't fire,
but came after me,

waving a tire jack.
I wore high heels,
couldn't run fast,
thought I was a goner.

Then a VW came along.
I lifted my handcuffed
hands and hollered.
It stopped for me.

I'm one of the lucky ones.
I've seen your picture
in all the newspapers—
No question, it was you.
I've seen your face
most nights in dreams,
big as the harvest moon,
grinning like a goon.

It's the good-looking
ones I distrust most—
the way they try to
sweet-talk their way.

Last week in a bar
a guy walked over,
touched my shoulder.
In the ladies' room

I puked my guts out.
I'll find one so homely
some day, I'll simply
go along with him, okay?

Fifteen years after,
you finally got fried.
Clean-shaven bastard,
inside me you're still alive.

II
Texas Cheerleader Murder Plot
Channelview, 1991

I, Wanda Webb Holloway, haven't asked for much.
I want to live in an all-white neighborhood
in a white house—no peeling paint for me.
I want the grass cut every week, whether it
needs it or not, and I want my house cleaned for me.
I want to be able to afford matching shoes
and handbags from Dillard's and I want the minister
to praise my organ playing on Sunday mornings.

So much for what I want for me. For my daughter,
my thirteen-year-old, I want more. Much more.
I want her to be popular with both girls and boys.
I want her to be the very center of attention.
I want her to be on the Channelview Cheerleading Squad.
I can see her leaping in the air, shaking her blue-
and-white pompoms, shaking her budding bubbies.
I can hear the stadium's roar when she jumps.

Problem is, she isn't blonde. It's as clear as
the nose on your face, they're partial to blondes.
Problem is, she's competing against the daughter
of that bitch who lives in a tract house like this,
hers is no better. My hair's bigger. She thinks
she's better, but she's not. Her bony blonde bitch daughter
doesn't even talk to my daughter at school.

So I have a plan. I don't have much money, but
I have my diamond earrings Buddy Lee gave me.
I'll barter them. I can give up my diamonds
to see that bitch wiped out. Not the daughter,
I mean the mother. If someone snuffs her mother
the night before the big tryouts at school,
that daughter will collapse in a puddle of grief.
I'll take the cheer right out of her leader.

Then my daughter will make the Squad. I have
a list, men willing to do the job. It's only
a matter of who and how. I'd like to snuff both
bitches, but I won't. Wanda Webb Holloway wouldn't
harm a child. I'd like to tell my daughter that
it's me who made her pompoms possible, but
I won't. I'd like to keep my diamonds, but
I won't. There's just no end to a mother.

Famous Last Words

for Dana Gioia

"It has all been very interesting!"
    declared Lady Mary Wortley Montague.
Examining his sickroom, Oscar Wilde railed,
    "Either that wallpaper goes, or I do."
Told the angels were waiting for him,
    Ethan Allen quipped, "Let 'em wait."
"I am so very happy," Gerard Manley Hopkins cooed.
    Goethe pleaded for "More light, more light."

Madame de Pompadour cried out to God,
    "Wait a minute!" rouged her cheeks red.
"I suppose I am turning into a god?"
    the dying Emperor Vespasian said.
Henry James, succumbing to a massive stroke,
    "So it has come . . . The Distinguished Thing."
Pancho Villa pleaded, "Don't let it end
    like this. Tell 'em I *said* something."

Gertrude to Alice B.: "What is the answer?"
    [Silence] "In that case, what is the question?"
"If this is dying, I don't think much of it,"
    muttered Lytton Strachey. When undone,
Julius Caesar managed, "Et tu, Brute?"
    Edmund Kean: "Dying is easy. Comedy is hard."
Chekhov: "It's been so long since I've had champagne."
    Goethe: "More light, more light," then departed.

Endymion and Selene

Floating over where Endymion slept,
the moon was stopped by his beauty,
could not help but kiss and fondle him.
So in love, she cast a spell—
she'd always know where to find him.
He never again awoke in that glade

to see the shining bending over him.
His beauty was his fate: he sleeps
forever, immortal but remote.
She left him on that mountain, dead
to daffodils, to every living thing,
yet warm and very much alive.

And what of Selene's fate? Nightly
she visits her lover, covers his face
with kisses. Still her passion
never can be satisfied. Her sighs
shake, make the crisp leaves crack.
And so it is with the two of us:

When you invite me up for a wine,
we cuddle on your couch. You lean
against me indifferently, enduring.
I always know where to find you.
You always let me caress you.
But I can never possess you.

My Funny Valentine

One in nine of all Valentines are sent by people to themselves.
—TV news item, February 14, 2002

Paula did it so others in the office—
who lunch at the Olive Garden together,
don't include her—won't think she is
a loser. On her desktop, it pulsates.

Sam sent himself six in varying sizes
and shades of red and pink. His secretary
(for whom he lusts in his heart and pants)
thinks him much sought-after, relents.

Angie did it to signal to her lover she
can't be taken for granted. She signed it
in block letters, black Magic Marker:
LUV YA FOREVER! YOUR ITALIAN STALLION!

Lester, who hardly gets any mail, subscribes
to seed—and Victoria's Secret—catalogues,
embraces junk mail, eats up fast-food flyers.
Today a scarlet letter quivers in his box.

Zoe, because all the mail she receives
is e-mail, longs for the tactility
of bond paper, scents of perfumed ink.
Where are the stamps of yesteryear?

Joe did it because his daughter disappeared
into a fog of dope and Haight-Ashbury.
She may be dead. He sent it inscribed,
"Your loving daughter as always, Hope."

Raby, because in elementary school,
when the teacher opened the Valentine Box
and called out names of recipients, he got
just one, addressed to Raby the Baby.

Emily, because she sent a letter
to the world that never wrote to her.
She lingers inside the hall for the post-
man to return her heart-shaped note.

I did it because I am, simply, absolutely,
madly in love with myself. Nobody does it
better than I do. And the best thing is,
I don't have to look my best.

Two for Max Eberts

I
Blue Jay

Generous gestures are so rare—
money unexpected in the mail,
a beautiful stranger's kiss,
a blue jay swooping down
on the birdbath this morning,
crying *Thief!*—visionary blue,
an angel's grace, heaven to see.

II
Trees in Springtime

Stirring at your extremities,
nodes twitch, push forth buds
which unfurl like the opening
of a hand. You never learn
to expect it. Suddenly your limbs
drop green filigree. No longer
teemless, your infant leaves
flutter-flutter like festival flags.
And birds return from wintering
in Miami to nestle in your boughs.

San Miguel de Allende

for Kathy and De Snodgrass

In the dining room at breakfast
I remark how carefully the butcher
has trimmed the bacon of all fat.

Someone at my table replies,
"This is Mexico, a poor country.
On the hogs there is no fat."

I think of American tourists
who walk the narrow streets,
their Rolexes and gold jewelry.

They pass squatting beggars, faces
dim as dying lightbulbs, selling
dusty candy, limp comic books.

All American women who live here
have face lifts, tummy tucks.
A discreet plastic surgeon

lives nearby, his Rolls picks them
up, delivers them to their doors.
"Old people go to Miami to die,

come to San Miguel to live."
The wives glow like warriors.
Flowers glow like brides.

At five A.M. my stone-walled
room still dark, I awake
to the first crows of cocks.

At noon it will be church bells,
at sundown all the dogs of San Miguel
will bark like dogs from hell.

Other sounds: a little band marches
before a crush of political banners.
Their bright uniforms color the tan

stone streets. How the natives love
brilliant hues—orange, grape, pink
grapefruit, saffron. From my balcony

I see the cocky young tuba player
has peroxided his black hair
metallic gold. Other colors—

royal blue and white ceramic tiles
behind my mantel, pomegranate shaped,
each a blue bird on a blue bowl,

each painted individually, each
different in a different way.
On the ancient stone mantelpiece,

a banana smiles before two tangerines.
On the table a calla lily thrives
in a glass of undrinkable water.

No television, no telephone, no radio
in my room, no classical music,
just mariachis roaming in restaurants.

Though it is January, it's still Christmas.
On the cathedral altar, Mary, Joseph,
Jesus, shepherds, wise men, a crucifix

entwined with Christmas tree lights
plus a gaudy blinking five-pointed star—
On, off. On, off. On, off. Worshipers,

women in black, Christians as hard as nails,
kneel on the stone floor. Tourists Kodak
snapshots. In the town's central square,

a crèche with carved wooden figures.
Before them, live animals penned in—
goat, calf, donkey, camel, cow.

One morning I hear a moving poetry reading
by a consummate American poet, bearded,
neglected in his own country, unlike

the turquoise and amethyst necklaces
I purchase for my wife for a pittance.
They will be greatly valued in the States.

I am driving to the countryside
to La Gruta Spa, invigorating hot water
springs enclosed in caves. I change,

enter a long rectangular pool
of tepid water, then make my way
to the far end, where I pass through

a long narrow dark tunnel of warmer
waters. As I work my way down
this dunkel tunnel, it seems as if

I am propelled down the birth canal.
I emerge into a deeper chamber
of hotter water—suddenly reborn.

I will be reluctant to leave San Miguel.
It is like dreaming vivid dreams,
and living them as well.

II A LITTLE LIGHT MUSIC

Memory

Memory is getting cheaper each day.

—Computer advertisement

Not in my case. It's getting more expensive.
        It costs more in effort, time, and spirit
to recall the title of the novel I want
        to recommend, where I last left
my checkbook, the name of that hot new bistro,
        what my wife needs from the supermarket.

When I can't remember in front of others,
        I attribute it to a Senior Moment—
though I'm not all that senior. At work they call
        me the Absent-Minded Professor. My mind
isn't absent, just needs some more memory to retrieve
        certain files. There's nothing wrong

with my long-term memory. I can recall
        my elementary school teachers—(first grade,
MISS ANNIE WARD! third grade, MISS RUTH WETZEL!
        fifth grade, MISS LIZZIE ANDERSON!).
I can even summon up the high school janitor,
        (MR. KEYES!), which is amusing,

because his ring clanked more keys than anyone's.
        I can recite all the stars of Republic Pictures
Westerns (LASH LARUE!), batting averages
        of the Dodgers, Giants; dates of World War II
battles. Now if only I could remember
        where I parked my car . . .

Life and Limb

Charlie Smith, the former slave believed
to be 137 years old, had his left leg
amputated below the knee in Lakeland, FL,
because of circulatory problems and was
reported in stable condition. He lost
his right leg below the knee in November 1977
for the same reason.

—*Los Angeles Times*

It's not easy being
137. I expected to lose
my hair, my sight,
my memory, my ability
to get it up. But, Christ!
Two limbs? I used to enjoy
shaking a leg. Lindy-ed
and fox-trotted. I tripped
the light fantastic till
I was 120. Now I can't
even trip. I don't have
a leg to stand on. They took
both away, they said,
to give me life—me
who already lived six score
and seventeen. What riles
me is, my left hand feels
numb. If I tell, they'll
prune the whole arm off
while I'm asleep some night.
And after that, they'll
saw off the right. I'll be
nothing but a human bowling

ball, or something to prop
open the door in the hall.
So here's my plan:
I'll run away.

Headlines

War Dims Hope for Peace.
Plane Too Close to Ground, Crash Probe Told.
Clinton Wins Budget; More Lies Ahead.

Miners Refuse to Work after Death.
Include Your Children When Baking Cookies.
War Dims Hope for Peace.

Something Went Wrong in Jet Crash, Experts Say.
Prostitutes Appeal to Pope.
Clinton Wins Budget; More Lies Ahead.

Local High School Dropouts Cut in Half.
Couple Slain; Police Suspect Homicide.
War Dims Hope for Peace.

Stolen Painting Found by Tree.
Panda Mating Fails; Veterinarian Takes Over.
Clinton Wins Budget; More Lies Ahead.

Iraqi Head Seeks Arms.
Police Campaign to Run Down Jaywalkers.
War Dims Hope for Peace.
Clinton Wins Budget; More Lies Ahead.

Miss Perfecto

She never admits to a mistake in her life,
and never will.

Like Saint Catherine of Alexandria, she was born
with a halo encircling her head.

Upbraids her office mates every workday,
asserting her superiority.

Opens personal mail addressed to others,
then discards it.

Rifles her assistant's desk drawers,
looking for "evidence."

Thinks she is gracious to her inferiors.
(Wherever does she find them?)

Believes she knows literature, can't tell
Ashbery from a dingleberry.

Orders her son to paint her office,
while she files her nails.

Demands her children wire birthday flowers,
gloats when they arrive.

Every phone call of such confidentiality,
she closes the door.

Goes to the gym to attempt to recover the body
her husband abandoned.

Is the dragon guarding the cave's mouth
in Wagner's *Siegfried*.

Is Mommy Dearest, screaming, "No more
wire clothes hangers!"

"Perfecto" is a cigar. At least it leaves
a good taste in one's mouth.

Response to Barbara Walters' Most Fatuous Question

Posed to Katharine Hepburn

If I could be any kind of tree,
what kind of tree would I be?

. . . Oh, a Live Oak, probably.
Soaring fifty feet triumphantly

toward heaven, limbs a filigree
extended even farther horizontally.

I'd stand faithful as Penelope,
shade for all who'd sit beneath me

all year round, because with sagacity
the Live Oak is an evergreen species.

I'd never experience the extremity
of winter, my kind grows southerly.

My acorns compounded annually,
I'd propagate a large family—

lots and lots of progeny
to line boulevards and allées.

I'd live well into antiquity,
a three-hundred-year expectancy,

which perhaps is long enough to see
all I've found I'd like to see.

And when I confront mortality,
ceasing mere ornamentality,

I'd unite beauty with utility
when they make lumber for a ship of me.

Soliloquy of the Ethiopian Eunuch

The miracle began with a miracle.
I was sitting in my gold-trimmed chariot
(well, not exactly *my* chariot—like all
my accoutrements, it belongs to *her*—
Candace, Queen of all the Ethiopians.
But since she put me in charge of her treasure,
I have the opportunity to live high.
Beauty has its privileges, and I don't mean
Candace. I'm here to tell you: that girl
Wasn't around when they passed out looks.)

There I was, biding my time in the chariot,
near Jerusalem where I'd gone to worship.
I'd just passed Gaza, a real cultural desert.
I was studying Isaiah the Prophet
when suddenly this white man was translated—
there's absolutely no other word for it—
he literally was *translated* from wherever
to right next to me. It was the damndest thing!
He just stood there, ahuffing and apuffing.
Then he says with the greatest impertinence,

"Do you understand that book you're reading?"
His meaning was undeniable: the fact
that I'm black must have implied I'm illiterate,
or ignorant at best, despite my purple
silk robe and heavily gilded chariot.
I said, "This Isaiah is a heavy dude.
Perhaps you can shed some light on this passage?"
He was led as a sheep to the slaughter;
and like a lamb dumb before her shearer,
so opened he not his mouth . . . "So who's the *he?*"

I asked. "Is this Isaiah talking
about himself, or is he palavering about
somebody else?" And Whitey (his real name was
Philip; it means Lover of Horses—ha!),
Whitey explained to me the "he" was Jesus,
and began to preach about the humiliation
of Jesus, and how his judgment was taken
away before his life on earth was taken,
and how he said not one word to save himself.
And now, in order to be saved, a body
must be baptized in the holy name of God.

I took it all in. Then he clambered inside
the chariot, and we commenced riding north,
which was where he came from before translated.
Presently we came upon a teensy pond.
"Here's some H_2O. So what's to keep you from
baptizing me on the spot?" That set him off
preaching some more: "If you believe with all
your heart that Jesus Christ is the Son of God,
blah blah blah, I'll do it." Seems this Jesus cat

charged him and a bunch of other honkeys
to preach all nations about this Jesus stuff.
I told him with my dusky skin I qualified as
"all nations." So I stopped the chariot,
and we both sashayed down to the water hole.
And hallelujah, he baptized me! In the name
of the Father, and the Son, and the Holy Ghost.
Like to drowned me. The waters of salvation
ran down my dreadlocks. My gloomy skin took on
a peaceful hue. My black soul became dove white.

Then that lover of horses disappeared—*Poof!*
It was enough to make my head spin, popping
in and out of the desert like that. Later
I heard Philip was preaching in this city
and that, creating real photo opportunities.
When I got back to the palace, I camped it up
about being saved, being washed in the blood
of the Lamb, and how this black soul now was white
as snow. (Though I confess I've never seen snow.
It's just one of those things you take on faith.)

Queen Candace had a hissy fit, stomped her foot
because she hadn't been baptized and her eunuch
had. I told her she'd just have to wait until
Philip or one of that gang of ten others
came her way. But she never did. I don't think
they thought hateful ugly queens much worth saving . . .
Now don't think being a eunuch is easy.
It was done so I could better serve my God
and my queen. I continued to lust in my heart.
But now I'm *saved*, I sleep the sleep of the just.

III RITUALS

Sunday Rituals

I

That silver gravy boat
was all afloat with giblets
till Father helped himself.
His ladle fished full fathom five.
Four children bated breaths,
waited, faces clean and wide
as china plates. We memorized
Father dipping—all the gizzard,
all the liver parts—then saw
the lonely heart get drowned
in his potato dam before he passed
the burgled gravy on.

II

    "The man of the family always carves,"
Mother rehearsed, cutting deeply into the rib roast.
She cast glances toward Father, who hunched
at the head of the table in the tallest chair,
Irish linen napkin tucked into the neck of his plaid
shirt. He claimed not to know how to carve.
    His smile was weak as water.

    "My father was an exquisite carver,"
she announced to assembled guests, or just to us
four kids waiting for interminable Sunday dinner
to end, Ed Sullivan's *Toast of the Town* to begin.
"He had a way with joints," she reminisced, trimming

away all the fat, slices falling one after another
like a stack of dominoes.

"He could carve a ham paper thin.
If you held a slice to the light, you could see
clear through." We children sniggered. Why would
anyone hold meat to the light? Why would how thin
it was make any difference in how it tastes?
She sawed away like a virtuoso cellist. Finally
    the knife struck bone.

"He was also a connoisseur of wine,
drove the finest horse and carriage in all Roanoke.
But I have always thought the true measure of a man
was how well he could carve." With that she lay
aside the ancestral carving knife, bestowed
a generous portion onto a Wedgewood plate, and passed
    Father the choicest cut.

Two for Mister Roscoe

I
"Arsh Potatoes"

"Roscoe's strictly a meat-and-potatoes man,"
was how Grandmother described my late grandfather.
There never was a dinner when we went over
without mashed potatoes—a smooth white mountain

heaped in a blue Willowware bowl. He always had thirds,
topped with gravy, which he called "The Essence."
After grace, he'd point: "Bobby, would you commence
to pass the Arsh potatoes?" His very words.

For years that's what I thought they were called—
not Irish potatoes, but Arsh. It was one
of the few things he got wrong. Farmer's son,
he dropped out in seventh grade to work. Prodigious

energies made successes of his tenant farms,
his timber lands, downtown stores, real estate.
Early he amassed a fortune in the aggregate,
was accorded great respect. With his charm

he was reelected Town Council president three
times. He was proud of his resemblance to Harry Truman,
and of his black Buicks, traded in every two
years. Last night we attended a black-tie Country

Club supper. "Country" club? That manicured fairway
in no way resembles the landscape he tamed in his youth.
So I smile, don't worry about being thought uncouth:
"Would you commence to pass the Arsh potatoes?" I say.

II
Grandfather's Cars

Every two years he traded them in ("As soon
as the ash trays get full") he said with good humor,
always a sedate four-door sedan, always a Buick,
always dark as the inside of a tomb.

Then one spring Grandfather took off to trade,
returned, parked proudly in the driveway.
"Shave-and-a-haircut, two bits!" blared the horn.
Grandmother emerged from the kitchen into day-

light, couldn't believe her eyes. Grandfather sat
behind the wheel of a tomato-red Lincoln
convertible, the top down. "Shave-and-a-haircut,
two bits!" "Roscoe, whatever were you thinking?"

she cried. Back into the kitchen she flew.
No matter how many times he leaned on that horn,
she wouldn't return. So he went inside,
found her decapitating strawberries with scorn.

"Katie, what's wrong with that automobile?
All my life I've wanted something sporty."
He stood there wearing his Montgomery Ward
brown suit and saddle shoes. His face was warty.

She wiped her hands along her apron,
said words that cut like a bandsaw:
"What ails you? They'll think you're turned fool!
All our friends are dying like flies—all!

You can't drive that thang in a funeral procession."
He knew she was right. He gave her one baleful
look, left, and returned in possession
of a four-door Dodge, black, practical as nails.
Grandfather hated that car until the day he died.

To a Schoolteacher Now Dead

"Bullfrog Henderson" we called you
behind your back, because of
hyperthyroid eyes, magnified
by glasses. Though you had not
seen me for thirty years, you'd have
called me by my Christian name.

You wrote, "Bobby is obstreperous!"
on my report card, and I thought
it a compliment, like "Bobby
is precocious," said before.
My parents informed me otherwise.
All elementary years blend,

but not the Fifth in your shadow,
the year I found an ancient
burial ground in some pasture.
Bones, shreds of purple cloth,
seen in a cracked crypt. I brought one
bone to class for Show and Tell.

I showed, you told: How you went on
about Desecration and Sacrilege!
I took the old brown hip bone
back where it belonged.
I did not understand the to-do.
You never told the owners of the plot.

You were bullfrog fat. Your operation
for hemorrhoids was talk of the school.
You brought a pillow to perch upon.
We made secret Fifth-Grade jokes

about "piles of money," "piles of snow,"
"piles of homework" you "piled upon us."

I remember best the gift you gave me,
the inexpressibly kind gift of a D
in arithmetic, long division,
doled out to a boy who always got an A.
You announced the grade to the class.
My hot-cheeked head hung like a cow's.
"I predict this will not happen again,"
you said (and it didn't). All the way
home that day I thought that D
was the tragic meaning of this life.
I thought of Father, the whipping I'd get,
allowance which would be suspended.

I hid the hateful report card
until they asked to see it. Produced,
I was astonished—Father smirked,
then broke into loud guffaws.
He could not contain his relief: His son
would not get straight A's in perpetuity.

Thank you, Miss Henderson, for putting me
in my place, for teaching me humility,
for giving me a D when surely I deserved
at least a C (maybe even a B?).
There is something to be said for overkill,
and Bullfrog Henderson, you were beautiful.

Viewing

They come, who have ever loved death
better than life, better than love
or the incantation of laughter,
delighting in the size of the floral
display, whispering how natural
the painted, powdered smile.

Two Sonnets

I
Her Life at Seven

And in the yard, before the open barn,
The girl would wait for Grandpa's Chevrolet
To turn, take her to town Saturday morns.
They'd shop, then have a chocolate nut sundae.

Sunday's they'd motor to the family plot.
She'd note the dates of relatives long gone:
"There's Roy, and Floyd, Hannah and Charlotte."
Homeward she'd nap curled in the backseat sun.

Some days her father came from the city,
Bringing his sad face and a stick of gum,
To tell her she was getting quite pretty,
Like her mother (who now was in "a home.")

No friends, no games, no sister or brother,
She grew up clear-eyed, herself or other.

II
Chance Encounter

If I should turn a corner of the street
And suddenly find you standing right there—
I'd grasp your hand, and see that our eyes meet.
I'd say, "How well you look. What lovely hair."
You'd say, "Are you still in the same old place?"
Your writing—has it entered a new phase?"

All the while I'm memorizing your face,
Then smile, create a parting of the ways.

A parting of the ways! When it did come,
Some fourteen years ago, it was as if
A hired assassin shot me with a gun,
Or a street urchin stuck me with a shiv.
I never thought I would get over it.
And I never let you discover it.

Days of 1964

They felt frightfully upper middle class,
moving into their Manhattan brownstone
third-floor apartment on East Thirty-sixth
—just two doors off Park. Their out-of-town
movables somehow fit into place:
ancestral sofa, new spinet piano,
glass-top table, white imitation French
Provincial bedroom set (their one mistake).

Floors were parquetry, ceilings fourteen feet
high, fireplace marble but, like the building's
"super," unfunctional. A crystal chandelier
Versailled the living room. They were long
on wicker, shutters, wrought iron, ferns,
short on cash. But credit was a soft touch
in those days. Plastic cards came unsolicited.
He strolled to work in a camel's hair topcoat
from Brooks, her hair was coiffed at Elizabeth Arden,
rinsed rather red. They were twenty-six.
She wore his pajama tops, he the bottoms.
(Once, taking out the garbage, they locked themselves
out wearing that stunning attire; they giggled
till the locksmith came.) They shared everything,
even an inordinate fondness for puns.
"With fronds like these, who needs anemones?"

Their tiny bathroom abutted their neighbors'.
Through the hot air vent they heard his laughter
morning and night. He laughed at everything
his wife said. They were older, European,
they made them models. Two years later,
winding past her on the staircase,

she volunteered, "Rainer and I are *kaput*!"
How could a marriage of laughter end?

They worried the question on their queen-size bed.
That was the year she became pregnant,
by December eight months gone. They pushed
the empty baby carriage up Murray Hill to relatives,
to gather all their Christmas presents.
They exalted in their elegant "shopping cart."
People stopped to see the baby, then chuckled
over the holiday packages inside. It snowed,
crystals glistened her long eyelashes.
He dashed out Saturday nights to buy the *Times.*
And now that their son is sixteen, they haven't lived
in that city for that many years. He goes
more or less his way, she goes hers,
strangers on a winding stair. Not exactly *kaput,*
perhaps, but something nearly so.
How could a marriage of laughter end?

The Ruined Man

To be a ruined man can be a vocation.

—T. S. Eliot on S. T. Coleridge

He had a vision, trained for it like an Olympian,
with absolute dedication, year out and year in.

At college he lost his scholarship in Engineering.
He managed that in one fall term and one spring.

His next feat was to marry and father a son,
then lose them both. This loss was hard won.

When he spoke, his voice emerged a thin mumble.
He lived in one rented room, his clothes a jungle.

He never put sheets on the bed, avoided the fuss.
He ate out of cans, not once put up a Christmas

tree. Visiting his small son, he gifted him
with a candy bar. His car had no chrome trim.

He applied for a little job in a big corporate
headquarters. On a slide rule he slid estimates

in the same cubicle for forty years. After eight
P.M. he haunted the Greyhound depot, calculating

why transients and travelers enter and egress,
strangers from Schenectady, Buffalo, Lake Success.

It was entertainment, He had nowhere else to go.
Winters in the city accumulated 120 inches of snow.

61

Inconspicuously hunched on a slat bench there,
he blew Camel rings into the air.

("He's just being a good Christian," his droll
schizophrenic son surmised. "It's in the Bible:

'It is easier for a Camel to go between
the Needle's Eye than a rich man to enter Heaven.'")

It took sixty-plus years to get it all undone,
eventually he destroyed throat, esophagus, and lungs.

When they claimed him to undergo the knife,
he took solace in the perfection of his life.

Bucolics

Mop and Nest

I
Neighbors drape their mop
        across the fence. It hangs,
worn-out, passed-out hag,

gray hair hanging down
        above the daffodil bed,
offense to any eye.

II
Each day a robin
        alights on it, pecks out
strands to weave in his nest—

testament to mans'
        absence of aesthetics, robins'
deft resourcefulness.

Wisteria and Fence

I
Without the fence, I'm grounded.
With the fence I soar, I bloom,
blossoms spilling like grapes,
lavendering the air with perfume.
With a wild love I wind
tendrils, adorn bare boards,
reaching, clinging, twining,
I grasp for my support.

II
This climber takes advantage,
its roots are undermining me.
Can't you see I'm already leaning
due to its ascendancy?
Some day I'll simply be crushed.
It's like affairs of the heart:
there's a lover and a beloved.
For god's sake, cut the upstart dead!

Insomnia

When he lived on the lonesome road
in the midst of the woods,
he slept deeply as a hibernating bear.

When he moved to the city
the sounds of traffic on cement
kept him awake all night.

Until he began to imagine
the noise was a soothing waterfall
over rocks. His sleeping resumed.

Two Adaptations from Red Pine

I
Waiting for a Friend
Chao Shih-Haiu, d. 1219

During magnolia season it rains on every vehicle
Mosquitoes swarm around swimming pools and spas
Waiting after midnight for a buddy who won't show
I throw darts with a stranger until closing time

II
Parting from a Friend on a Night in Spring
Ch'en Tzu-Ang, d. 702

While orange smoke insinuates from Pasadena
We raise longnecks in the Ice House
Thoughts like guitars Friday nights
Following an interminable Interstate
The lurid moon goes down on oil derricks
The Big Dipper hangs it up at dawn
The road to Wichita Falls runs so far away
What year will it turn and run back again

Red Pine is the pen name of writer and scholar Bill Porter,
one of the world's most respected translators of Chinese
literature.

Christopher Isherwood

Not only a single man,
but a singular man.

Also several men: Christopher
who visits Mister Lancaster,

Christopher, with Ambrose who wiles
every summer on his Greek isle,

Christopher in Berlin with Sally Bowles,
Christopher who was a camera and consoler.

Christopher witnessing the Munich crisis,
Christopher with Don in California places.

Not to mention the middle-aged writer.
For all these magical Christophers,

We readers are grateful, he
informs us of who we might be.

He used homosexuals as metaphors
for all people some deplore.

Among gay novels, *A Single Man*
is still one of the best.

In *Down There on a Visit* he heard
the voices of the nether world.

In that book, when he took the outboard
engine, had it fall into the water,

It's easily retrieved, the water
so shallow. Herr Ishyvoo was never shallow.

Cyril Connolly described his work
as "fatal readability." Isherwood

The writer made what's hard look easy.

Vita

Worked at the wrong job
        for twenty-nine years,
makes up for lost time.

Wears a tie to teach.
        Can't get their respect one way,
get it another.

Feels good when he's had
        a close haircut. Memories
of a grape lollipop.

Drives a fifteen-year-
        old car. "In another five,
it'll be a classic!"

Won't use a computer, has
        one of the finest minds of
the nineteenth century.

Hates most holidays,
        because they mean there'll be no
mail delivery.

Remembers birthdays
        of all friends and relatives,
lonely on his own.

Won't tolerate sham,
        like televangelists
pocketing fortunes.

Secretly depressed
        whenever short of money,
but gives a lot away.

Gets upset when guests
        stain tabletops with glasses
when there are coasters.

Likes to cook, has found
        The Frugal Gourmet neither
frugal nor gourmet.

Is envious of
        men who can refold roadmaps,
homes with huge kitchens.

Gets angry when friends
        keep him waiting half an hour
in a restaurant.

Likes well-tailored suits,
        knows on him they resemble
someone's unmade bed.

Roughing it, for him,
        means turning the electric
blanket down to Five.

Terrible arthritis.
        His back feels like a bag of
broken dog biscuits.

Hates it when his aunt,
    who won't use a hearing aid,
tells him he's mumbling.

His prince of a son
    has begun to forgive him,
almost, everything.

Most beautiful pet
    he'd had? A cat with an a-
symmetrical face.

First sex was better
    than it ever got. Since then,
downhill all the way.

His wife's a comfort.
    Oh yes, his wife comforts him.
Like a cold pizza.

Three things he'd wish for:
    good looks, millions in the bank,
a humungous dick.

One concept escapes
    his experience totally—
the idea of fun.

At age sixty-four,
    still waiting for his Dad's shout:
"Son, let's go play catch!"

A pulled back kept him
         from his father's funeral.
Psychosomatic?

Never saw a ghost,
         but thinks he heard one, midnight
in dead grandparents' house.

Believes there's a God,
         yet only graces the church
Christmas and Easter.

A lousy patient.
         When he falls mortally ill,
please pull that damned plug.

This is Robert Phillips's seventh full-length book of poems. His poetry has won an Award in Literature from the American Academy of Arts and Letters, a Creative Artists' Public Service Award from New York State, and a Pushcart Prize, among others. He is a former chancellor of the Texas Institute of Letters. He lives with his wife in Houston, where he has been Director of the Creative Writing Program at the University of Houston. He now teaches as a John and Rebecca Moores Professor at the university. He is the literary executor of the American poets Delmore Schwartz and Karl Shapiro and has edited eight volumes of their works.

POETRY TITLES IN THE SERIES

John Hollander, *"Blue Wine" and Other Poems*
Robert Pack, *Waking to My Name: New and Selected Poems*
Philip Dacey, *The Boy under the Bed*
Wyatt Prunty, *The Times Between*
Barry Spacks, *Spacks Street: New and Selected Poems*
Gibbons Ruark, *Keeping Company*
David St. John, *Hush*
Wyatt Prunty, *What Women Know, What Men Believe*
Adrien Stoutenberg, *Land of Superior Mirages: New and
    Selected Poems*
John Hollander, *In Time and Place*
Charles Martin, *Steal the Bacon*
John Bricuth, *The Heisenberg Variations*
Tom Disch, *Yes, Let's: New and Selected Poems*
Wyatt Prunty, *Balance as Belief*
Tom Disch, *Dark Verses and Light*
Thomas Carper, *Fiddle Lane*
Emily Grosholz, *Eden*
X. J. Kennedy, *Dark Horses*
Wyatt Prunty, *The Run of the House*
Robert Phillips, *Breakdown Lane*
Vicki Hearne, *The Parts of Light*
Timothy Steele, *The Color Wheel*
Josephine Jacobsen, *In the Crevice of Time: New and
    Collected Poems*
Thomas Carper, *From Nature*
John Burt, *Work without Hope*
Charles Martin, *What the Darkness Proposes*
Wyatt Prunty, *Since the Noon Mail Stopped*
William Jay Smith, *The World below the Window: Poems, 1937–1997*
Wyatt Prunty, *Unarmed and Dangerous: New and Selected Poems*
Robert Phillips, *Spinach Days*
John T. Irwin, ed. *Words Brushed by Music: Twenty-five Years of
    the Johns Hopkins Poetry Series*
John Bricuth, *As Long As It's Big: A Narrative Poem*
Robert Phillips, *Circumstances Beyond Our Control: Poems*